LET'S FIND OUT! THE HUMAN BODY

THE BRAIN IN YOUR BODY

BRIDGET HEOS

Britannica
Educational Publishing

IN ASSOCIATION WITH

ROSEN
EDUCATIONAL SERVICES

T0082223

Published in 2015 by Britannica Educational Publishing (a trademark of Encyclopædia Britannica, Inc.) in association with The Rosen Publishing Group, Inc.
29 East 21st Street, New York, NY 10010

Copyright © 2015 The Rosen Publishing Group, Inc. and Encyclopædia Britannica, Inc. Encyclopædia Britannica, Britannica, and the Thistle logo are registered trademarks of Encyclopædia Britannica, Inc. All rights reserved.

Distributed exclusively by Rosen Publishing.
To see additional Britannica Educational Publishing titles, go to rosenpublishing.com

First Edition

Britannica Educational Publishing
J.E. Luebering: Director, Core Reference Group
Mary Rose McCudden: Editor, Britannica Student Encyclopedia

Rosen Publishing
Hope Lourie Killcoyne: Executive Editor
Jacob R. Steinberg: Editor
Nelson Sá: Art Director
Brian Garvey: Designer
Cindy Reiman: Photography Manager

Cataloging-in-Publication Data

Heos, Bridget, author.
The brain in your body/Bridget Heos.—First edition.
    pages cm.—(Let's find out! The human body)
Includes bibliographical references and index.
ISBN 978-1-62275-636-0 (library bound)—ISBN 978-1-62275-637-7 (pbk.)—ISBN 978-1-62275-638-4 (6-pack)
1. Brain—Juvenile literature. 2. Human body—Juvenile literature. 3. Human physiology—Juvenile literature. I. Title.
QP376.H33 2015
612.8'2—dc23

2014020156

Manufactured in the United States of America.

Photo Credits: Cover, p. 1 © iStockphoto.com/RapidEye; interior pages background © iStockphoto.com/Firstsignal; pp. 4, 5, 8-9 (bottom), 10, 22, 25 Encyclopædia Britannica, Inc.; p. 6 moodboard/Thinkstock; p. 7 Blamb/Shutterstock.com; p. 9 (top) Anthony Correia/Shutterstock.com; p. 11 Dorling Kindersley/Thinkstock; p. 12 Original preparation by J. Klingler, Anatomical Museum, Basel, Switzerland; p. 13 Annaick Kermoal/Science Source; pp. 14, 16, 18 Roger Harris/Science Source; p. 15 BISP/Universal Images Group/Getty Images; p. 17 © Rubberball Productions/Getty Images; p. 19 Odua Images; p. 20 © Merriam-Webster Inc.; pp. 20-21 Professor P. M. Motta and D. Palermo/Science Source; p. 23 Mike Agliolo/Science Source; pp. 24-25 Purestock/Thinkstock; p. 26 ArtyVectors/iStock/Thinkstock; p. 27 Sergiy Zavgorodny/Shutterstock.com; p. 28 © AP Images; p. 29 © Photodisc/Thinkstock.

CONTENTS

WHAT IS THE BRAIN?

The brain is the organ that controls how all parts of your body work. It also controls your thoughts and feelings. The brain allows you to sense the outside world. The brain helps your body stay healthy and respond in the right way to its environment.

The brain is connected to the spinal cord. The spinal cord contains nerves that run to

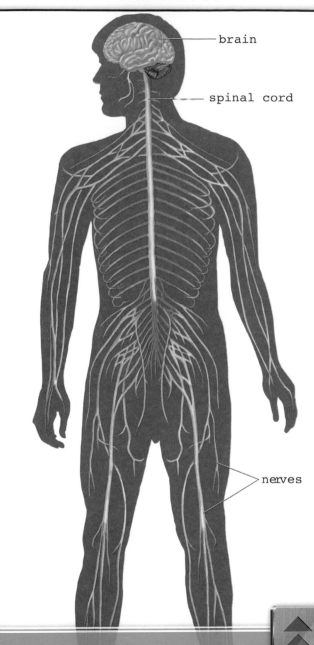

brain

spinal cord

nerves

The nervous system allows the brain to communicate with the body. The nervous system is made up of the brain, the spinal cord, and nerves.

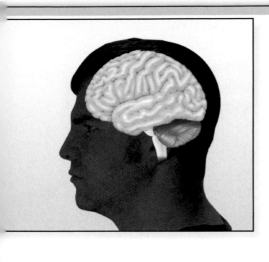

cerebrum

cerebellum

brain stem

The human brain has three main parts: the cerebrum, the cerebellum, and the brain stem. Together they control how all parts of the human body work.

and from the brain. These nerves carry messages between the brain and the rest of the body. Together the brain, spinal cord, and nerves make up the nervous system.

The three main parts of the brain are called the cerebrum, the cerebellum, and the brain stem.

The **nervous system** processes information about the outside world as well as the inner workings of your body. The nerves send the information to the brain, which makes sense of the information. The brain then sends a message back through the nerves to tell the body how to react.

THE BRAIN STEM

The brain looks something like a mushroom. The "stem" of the mushroom is the brain stem. The brain stem is attached to the spinal cord. The brain stem controls the things that happen automatically in the body. This includes feeling hungry or thirsty or getting sleepy.

The lower part of the brain stem is called the medulla oblongata, or just medulla. The medulla controls important processes such as heartbeat and breathing. It also sends signals between the spinal cord and the upper parts of the brain.

Blood pressure tells us how strong the heart is beating. During a health checkup, the nurse checks a patient's blood pressure. Blood pressure is regulated by the medulla.

The medulla controls heartbeat, breathing, and other automatic processes. The pons is located above the medulla on the brain stem. It controls feeling in the face.

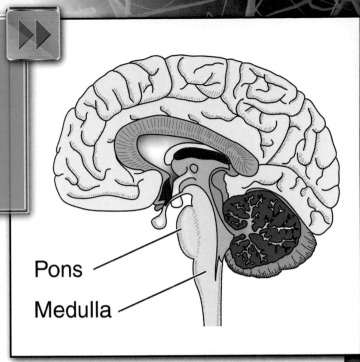

Pons

Medulla

THINK ABOUT IT

The brain stem controls automatic processes in the body such as hunger. Automatic processes are things that we cannot control. What are some other automatic processes that happen in our bodies?

Above the medulla is a part of the brain called the pons. The pons is associated with feeling in the face. The upper part of the brain stem is the midbrain. The midbrain helps with muscle control and eye movement. At the top of the brain stem are structures that control pleasure, pain, hunger, thirst, and body temperature. They also act as the relay center for all of the senses except smell and sight.

THE CEREBELLUM

The cerebellum is located just below and behind the brain stem and the cerebrum. It is much smaller than the cerebrum, but it has as many nerve cells as there are in all the other regions of the brain combined.

The cerebellum controls body movement. It is the part of the brain that allows people to learn motor skills. Unlike automatic processes, motor skills are movements that you decide to make. They include walking, skipping, and throwing a ball.

The cerebellum also helps people speak. Somebody with an injured cerebellum

The cerebellum is located behind the brain stem. It allows people to learn new motor skills, such as running, skipping, and dancing.

Motor skills are physical movements that a person decides to make. How are motor skills different from automatic processes?

When a pitcher throws a ball he is using the part of the brain called the cerebellum. The cerebellum controls the movement of the muscles in his arms and legs to line up and throw a perfect pitch.

pons

medulla oblongata

cerebellum

might have slow speech. He or she might also slur words.

9

THE CEREBRUM

If the brain is something like a mushroom, the cerebrum is the "cap" of the mushroom. It accounts for two-thirds of the total weight of the brain. The cerebrum is the part of the brain that controls thinking. It also controls many other functions.

The cerebrum is divided into two **cerebral hemispheres**, or halves. The left hemisphere actually controls the right side

Lobes of the brain

parietal lobe   frontal lobe

occipital lobe   temporal lobe

The cerebrum controls thinking. It is made up of four lobes, or sections, that control different kinds of thought.

A **cerebral hemisphere** is either of the two halves of the cerebrum. The two halves are divided by a long fissure or separation.

of the body. The right hemisphere, in turn, controls the left side of the body.

The two halves work together, but sometimes one half has more control over certain activities than the other half. For example, for some people the left side seems to control language and speech while the right side controls emotions.

The two halves of the brain are separated by a deep groove. At the base of the groove is a bundle of nerves that allows the two halves to communicate and to work together.

Inside the Cerebral Hemispheres

Each hemisphere of the brain has an outer layer and an inner core. The outer layer is made up of material called gray matter. The inner core is made up of white matter. The gray matter is where thinking occurs. It is also where information is stored. The white matter helps with communication between different areas in the gray matter.

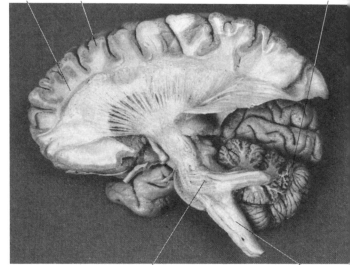

white matter   gray matter   cerebellum

pons   medulla oblongata

This photo shows one half of the brain—the left hemisphere. The darker outer layer is the gray matter, and the lighter inner core is the white matter.

The outer layer, or gray matter, is also called the cortex. The cerebral cortex has wrinkled ridges. These ridges are called gyri. They make the brain appear lumpy. "Sulci" is the name for the grooves between the gyri. The two most important sulci divide the brain into four sections, called lobes. These lobes are called the frontal, parietal, temporal, and occipital lobes.

THINK ABOUT IT

Sometimes in science, words have strange spellings or unusual forms. All the grooves in the brain together are called sulci (pronounced "sul-sigh"), but each individual groove is called a sulcus ("sul-kus"). All the ridges together are called gyri ("jai-rai"). What do you think we call each individual ridge?

The outer layer of the cerebrum has ridges called gyri. The grooves between the ridges are called sulci.

THE FRONT OF THE BRAIN

The frontal lobe is in the front part of the brain, behind the forehead. It is the largest of the four lobes. One of its jobs is to control a variety of movements. Damage to this area can result in weakness or paralysis on the opposite side of the body. Paralysis means that you cannot move your muscles.

The frontal lobe controls your conscience — the sense of what is right and what is wrong.

In 1848, a railroad worker named Phineas Gage had an accident, and a metal bar went through the frontal lobe of his brain. He survived, but the loss of parts of his frontal lobe changed his personality.

The frontal lobe also helps you understand the difference between right and wrong. It allows you to think about your actions and to make choices about how to behave. Knowing right from wrong and the feeling that you should do what is right is called your conscience.

THINK ABOUT IT

When was the last time you wanted to do something, but knew you might get in trouble if you did? That was your frontal lobe at work!

WHERE WE FEEL

The **parietal** ("puh-rie-i-tul") lobe is behind the frontal lobe. It contains the part of your brain that "feels" things. When you touch ice, scrape your knee, or pet a dog, the parietal lobe is where you feel these senses. Because of this lobe, you can detect the cold temperature of ice or the furry texture of a dog.

The parietal lobe is located behind the frontal lobe. When you touch something or hurt yourself, this part of the brain is activated.

The parietal lobe is also important in understanding language. Another one of its key tasks is awareness of your body and the space around it. A person with injuries to the parietal lobe may not understand the space around him or her well. For example, he or she may eat only the food on the right half of his or her plate.

Is this dog's fur soft or rough? Warm or cold? Wet or dry? The parietal lobe helps you understand this type of information.

Parietal is used to describe the parts of your body near the upper back wall of your head. It comes from a Latin word that means "of walls."

Memory and Vision Centers

The temporal lobes are located on the sides of the brain. They help process sounds and memories. A sea horse-shaped area in the temporal lobe called the hippocampus is where short-term memories become long-term memories. Short-term memory is our ability to remember

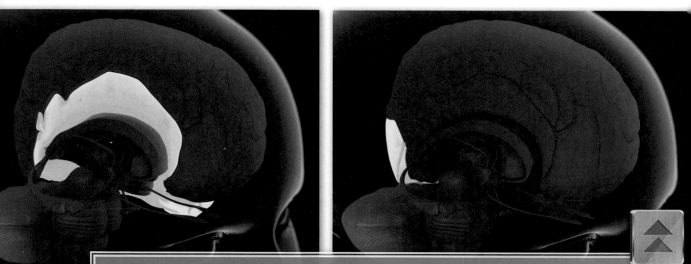

When a person remembers something that happened long ago, he or she is using the hippocampus. The hippocampus is located in the temporal lobe *(left)*. The occipital lobe *(right)* lies at the back of the brain.

THINK ABOUT IT

Alzheimer disease is an illness that attacks nerve cells in the brain. Patients with Alzheimer disease usually lose some of their memory. If Alzheimer disease affects your memory, which part of the brain do you think it attacks?

new information, such as the name of somebody we just met. Long-term memory is our ability to remember that information for a very long time, even years later!

The occipital ("ok-sip-it-ul") lobe is at the back of the brain. It is the visual center of the brain. The occipital lobe is where humans make sense of what they see. In the occipital lobe, signals from the eyes go through complex changes. After these changes, the brain can understand what the eyes are seeing.

The eye may be able to see things, but it's the brain that makes sense of what is seen, and that happens in the occipital lobe.

BRAIN CELLS

The human brain has two main types of cells: nerve cells, called neurons, and neuroglia. The neurons transport information. These cells are the basic working unit of the nervous system. Each neuron has parts that carry messages to and from the brain. These parts are

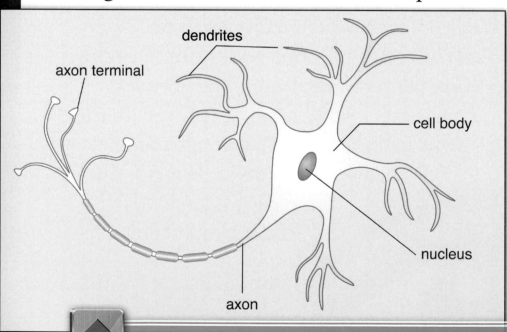

dendrites

axon terminal

cell body

nucleus

axon

Brain cells called neurons carry messages through the brain. Axons carry information away from the neuron to other cells. Dendrites accept information from the axons of other cells and carry it into the neuron.

THINK ABOUT IT

Scientists once thought that people were born with all the neurons they would ever have in life. Now they think people might produce some new neurons during their lifetime. Losing neurons causes memory loss and dementia. Why is it helpful for scientists to discover how we make new neurons?

called the axon and dendrites. The other type of cells are neuroglia. The neuroglia provide a protective environment for the neurons.

The brain contains about 100 billion neurons. We lose about 200,000 neurons each day! Because we have so many neurons, we don't notice the loss until we are very old. At that point, many people start to lose their memory or suffer from dementia. A person who has dementia cannot think clearly, understand, or remember.

We have many more neuroglia than neurons in our brains. The neuroglia provide an environment that helps neurons send and receive messages quickly.

THE INFORMATION FACTORY

The brain is like an information factory. Information is transferred along chains of interconnected neurons. Each neuron consists of a cell body with branches called dendrites and axons. Axons carry information away from the cell body. Dendrites carry information to the cell body.

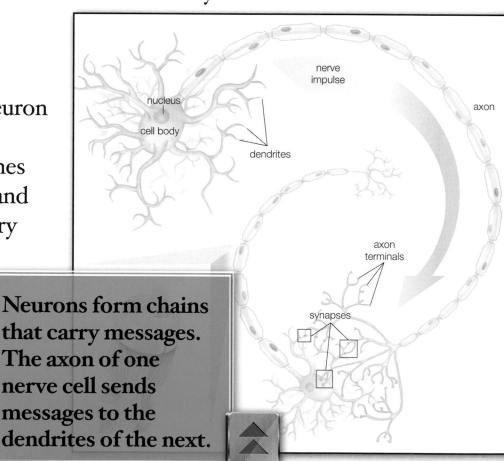

nucleus

cell body

dendrites

nerve impulse

axon

axon terminals

synapses

Neurons form chains that carry messages. The axon of one nerve cell sends messages to the dendrites of the next.

The gap between an axon and dendrite is called a synapse. Messages cross this synapse through an electrochemical process.

The transfer of information is an **electrochemical** process. An electrical impulse travels from the cell body through the axon. There is a small gap, called a synapse, between the axon of one neuron and the dendrite of the next neuron. At the end of the axon, there are tiny sacs that contain chemicals called neurotransmitters. When the electrical impulse reaches these sacs, they send neurotransmitters into the synapse. This sparks an electrical impulse in the next neuron.

Electrochemical processes change electrical energy into chemical energy, or the other way around.

THE BRAIN AND THE BODY

The spinal cord carries messages between the brain and the rest of the body. The spinal cord is made up of nerves. Nerves are cord-like collections of neurons. Nerves also branch out from the spinal cord and run throughout the whole body. There are two main types of nerves. Sensory nerves send information from the mouth, nose, skin, and other body parts to the spinal cord and brain. Motor nerves send information from the brain and spinal cord to the muscles and other body parts.

The spinal cord carries messages between the brain and body. The spinal cord is made up of nerves, and it is protected by the backbone.

COMPARE AND CONTRAST

When you step on something sharp, sensory nerves run to the brain and yell, "Ouch!" Motor nerves then tell you to lift your foot. In what ways are sensory nerves and motor nerves similar? What is one major difference in their jobs?

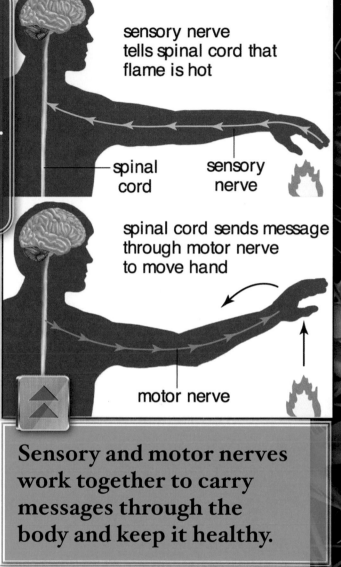

sensory nerve tells spinal cord that flame is hot

spinal cord

sensory nerve

spinal cord sends message through motor nerve to move hand

motor nerve

Sensory and motor nerves work together to carry messages through the body and keep it healthy.

All of these nerves work together to protect the body and keep it working properly. For example, when a person touches a hot stove, the sensory nerves in the fingers send impulses to the spinal cord. The impulses say that the stove is too hot to touch. The spinal cord then sends impulses through motor nerves to the muscles of the arm. These impulses tell the muscles to pull the arm away from the stove.

Our Natural Helmet

The brain has a natural helmet that protects it. This helmet is made up of the skull and three membranes, or coverings, that surround the brain. The outer membrane is called the dura mater (which means "hard mother"). It is tough and fibrous. The middle membrane is called the arachnoid. The arachnoid is thin and weblike. The

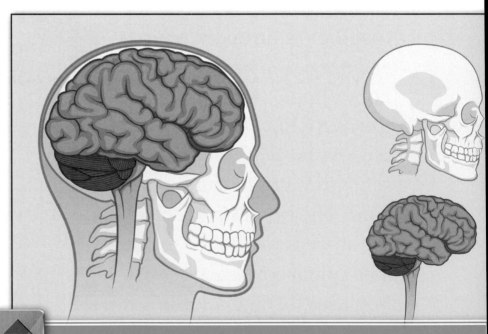

The skull and three membranes work together to form a helmet that protects the brain.

The brain is protected by a natural helmet. However, the skull cannot protect the brain from all injuries, so it is important to wear a helmet when skating, biking, or playing other sports.

inner covering is called the pia mater ("tender mother"). The pia mater is a delicate membrane that covers the surface of the brain.

Between the pia mater and arachnoid is a clear liquid. The brain floats in this liquid. This fluid is slippery and takes in shock. Like a helmet, it protects the brain from blows. It also brings nutrients to the brain. This fluid also surrounds the spinal cord.

COMPARE AND CONTRAST

The skull is a layer of bone that serves as an outer protection for the brain. Compare and contrast the skull and the liquid that surrounds the brain. How are they different?

Brain Injuries and Disorders

Even though it is protected, the brain can become injured. Hits to the head can cause serious injury. A brain can also be damaged if it does not receive enough blood because of a stroke or other condition. Depending on which part of the brain is injured, a person can have physical disabilities, problems with the senses, or changes in thought and behavior.

Brain injuries can happen while playing sports or during a car accident. After any hit to the head, it's important to see a doctor and make sure your brain is not injured.

The bright blue area at the bottom right side of this image is a brain tumor. Brain tumors are caused by uncontrolled growth of brain cells.

The brain can also suffer from infections and diseases such as cancer. Other diseases, such as epilepsy, can be caused by problems with the electrical impulses in the brain.

Because of its key part in thinking and controlling the body, the brain is one of our most important organs. Thankfully, science keeps finding new ways to keep it healthy and to fix injuries. That's good news, because a healthy brain means a healthy body!

Epilepsy is a medical condition in the brain in which brain cells fire electrical signals too quickly. Too many signals cause seizures, or twitching muscles.

Glossary

Alzheimer disease An illness that attacks nerve cells in the brain, causing loss of memory.

axon A strand of a neuron that carries nerve impulses away from the cell body.

brain stem The back and lower part of the brain including the midbrain, pons, and medulla oblongata.

cerebellum A large portion of the back part of the brain that controls body movement and speech.

cerebrum The part of the brain that controls thinking.

cortex The outer layer of gray matter on the cerebrum.

dendrite A strand of a neuron that carries nerve impulses toward the cell body.

lobe A rounded part of an organ in the body.

membrane A flexible sheet or layer, especially of a plant or animal part.

motor skill A learned movement of the muscles done on purpose.

nerve One of the stringy bands of tissue that connects the nervous system with other organs and carries nerve impulses.

nerve impulses Changes in electrical charges that move through the nervous system to carry messages between body parts and the brain.

nervous system The network of nerves and the brain in your body.

neuroglia Cells that protect neurons in the brain.

neuron A nerve cell; the basic working unit of the nervous system.

skull The case of bone that forms the skeleton of the head and surrounds the brain.

spinal cord The cord of nervous tissue that extends from the brain along the back.

For More Information

Books

Deak, JoAnn, and Sarah Ackerley. *Your Fantastic Elastic Brain*. San Francisco, CA: Little Pickle Press, 2010.

Halvorson, Karin. *Inside the Brain*. Minneapolis, MN: ABDO Publishing, 2013.

Schnurbush, Barbara. *Striped Shirts and Flowered Pants: A Story about Alzheimer's Disease for Young Children*. Washington, DC: Magination Press, 2007.

Stewart, Melissa. *How Is My Brain Like a Supercomputer? And Other Questions About the Human Body*. New York, NY: Sterling Children's Books, 2014.

Strange, Christopher M. *The Brain Explained*. New York, NY: Rosen Publishing, 2014.

Websites

Because of the changing nature of Internet links, Rosen Publishing has developed an online list of websites related to the subject of this book. This site is updated regularly. Please use this link to access this list:

http://www.rosenlinks.com/LFO/Brain

INDEX

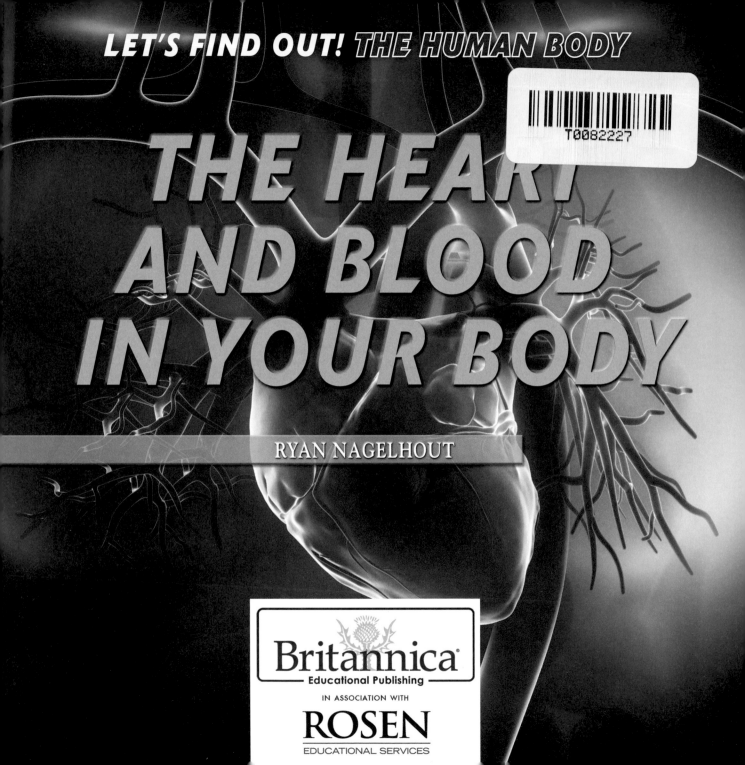

THE HEART AND BLOOD IN YOUR BODY

RYAN NAGELHOUT

Britannica
Educational Publishing

IN ASSOCIATION WITH

ROSEN
EDUCATIONAL SERVICES

Published in 2015 by Britannica Educational Publishing (a trademark of Encyclopædia Britannica, Inc.) in association with The Rosen Publishing Group, Inc.
29 East 21st Street, New York, NY 10010

Copyright © 2015 by Encyclopædia Britannica, Inc., Britannica, Encyclopædia Britannica, and the Thistle logo are registered trademarks of Encyclopædia Britannica, Inc. All rights reserved.

Distributed exclusively by Rosen Publishing.
To see additional Britannica Educational Publishing titles, go to rosenpublishing.com.

First Edition

Britannica Educational Publishing
J.E. Luebering: Director, Core Reference Group
Mary Rose McCudden: Editor, Britannica Student Encyclopedia

Rosen Publishing
Hope Lourie Killcoyne: Executive Editor
Kathy Kuhtz Campbell: Senior Editor
Nelson Sá: Art Director
Michael Moy: Designer
Cindy Reiman: Photography Manager

Library of Congress Cataloging-in-Publication Data

Nagelhout, Ryan, author.
The heart and blood in your body/Ryan Nagelhout.   First edition.
    pages cm. — (Let's find out! The human body)
Audience: Grades 3 to 6.
Includes bibliographical references and index.
ISBN 978-1-62275-640-7 (library bound) — ISBN 978-1-62275-641-4 (pbk.) —
ISBN 978-1-62275-642-1 (6-pack)
1. Cardiovascular system — Juvenile literature. 2. Blood — Juvenile literature. 3. Human body — Juvenile literature. 4. Human physiology — Juvenile literature. [1. Circulatory system.] I. Title.
QP103.N34 2015
612.1 — dc23
                                                                                    2014021405
Manufactured in the United States of America

Photo Credits: Cover © iStockphoto.com/Eraxion; p. 1, interior pages background Cliparea Custom media/Shutterstock.com; pp. 4 Science Photo Library/Pixologicstudio/Brand X Pictures/Getty Images; pp. 5, 7 Dorling Kindersley/Getty Images; p. 6 Science Photo Library/Sciepro/Brand X Pictures/Getty Images; pp. 8, 9, 10, 12, 15, 17, 28 Encyclopædia Britannica, Inc.; p. 11 Science Photo Library/Punchstock; p. 13 BSIP/Universal Images Group/Getty Images; p. 14 Science Photo Library/Steve Gschmeissner/Getty Images; p. 16 Biology Media/Photo Researchers/Getty Images; p. 18 Ed Reschke/Photolibrary/Getty Images; p. 19 David Mack/Science Photo Library/Getty Images; p. 20 National Cancer Institute/Science Photo Library/Getty Images; p. 21 David Long/E+/Getty Images; p. 22 Tek Image/Science Photo Library/Getty Images; p. 23 Pixologicstudio/Science Photo Library/Getty Images; p. 24 Hank Morgan/Photo Researchers/Getty Images; p. 25 Darrin Klimek/Digital Vision/Thinkstock; p. 26 Spencer Grant/Photo Researchers/Getty Images.

CONTENTS

Introducing The Heart

If you sit still and put a hand on your chest, you can feel something thumping. You can even hear it if you listen carefully. The organ inside your chest making that noise is your heart.

The human heart is one of the most

The heart is always working to keep the body alive.

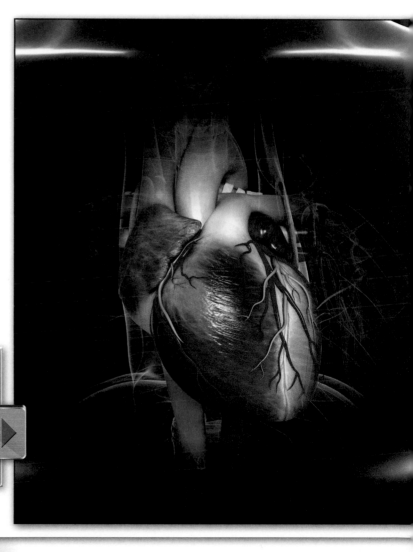

An **organ** is a part of
a person that consists
of cells and tissues and
performs particular tasks.

important organs in the
body. It pumps blood to every
other organ, which helps move
nutrients and wastes through the body.
The blood moves through a system of
tubes called vessels. Together, the heart
and the blood vessels make up the body's
cardiovascular system.

The heart pumps blood
through a vast network
of different kinds of
blood vessels.

THE HUMAN HEART

The heart is a muscle about the size of a person's fist. It is pear shaped and sits high in the chest, slightly to the left. As humans grow larger, the heart grows along with the body. The heart is made of very strong muscle. This muscle pumps blood by squeezing and relaxing in a regular rhythm. This rhythm is called the heartbeat.

A heart of an adult weighs about 8 to 12 ounces (230 to 340 grams).

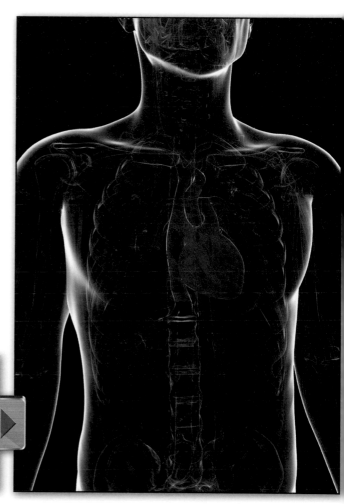

THINK ABOUT IT

The heart in a normal body at rest beats anywhere from 60 to 100 times per minute. What makes a heart beat faster?

Blood is the life fluid of the human body and the liquid that transports nutrients and removes waste. Blood travels from the heart to the lungs. In the lungs, blood releases carbon dioxide and takes in oxygen. The blood returns to the heart, where it is pumped throughout the body.

More than 4 quarts (3.8 liters) of blood pass through the heart every minute.

DIVIDING IT UP

The human heart is divided into right and left halves. Each half is divided into two hollow sections called chambers. The upper chambers are called atria (plural for atrium). The lower chambers are called ventricles.

Blood from the body flows into the right atrium. The blood then passes into the right ventricle, which pumps the blood to the lungs. In the lungs, blood picks up oxygen and releases **carbon dioxide**.

The heart muscle's fibers form a structure like a net. These fibers form the chambers of the heart.

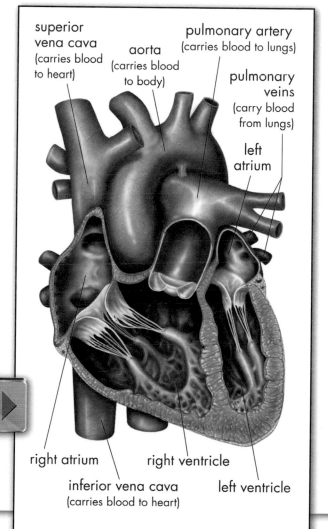

superior vena cava (carries blood to heart)

aorta (carries blood to body)

pulmonary artery (carries blood to lungs)

pulmonary veins (carry blood from lungs)

left atrium

right atrium

inferior vena cava (carries blood to heart)

right ventricle

left ventricle

Carbon dioxide is a gas that human cells make as waste. It is sent to the lungs and removed from the body when a person breathes out.

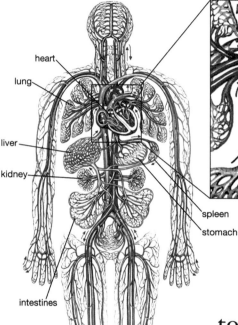

heart

lung

liver

kidney

spleen

stomach

intestines

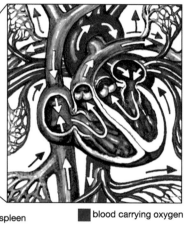

■ blood carrying oxygen

■ blood with no oxygen

The oxygen-rich blood enters the heart's left atrium. The blood then passes into the left ventricle. The left ventricle pumps the blood to the aorta, the main blood vessel that carries blood to all other parts of the body.

Blood without oxygen enters the heart's right side. It is returned to the heart's left side after taking up oxygen in the lungs.

DOING SOME CARDIO

The heart is the main organ in the cardiovascular system. A network of blood vessels makes up the rest of the system. Blood vessels are hollow tubes that carry blood throughout the body. Blood vessels are different sizes and

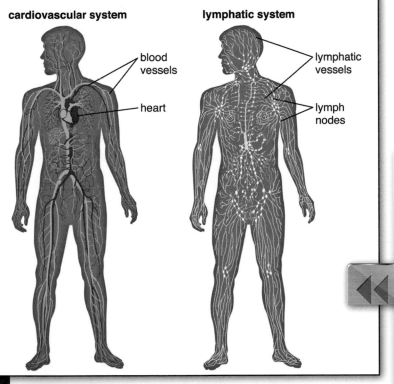

Circulatory system

cardiovascular system

blood vessels

heart

lymphatic system

lymphatic vessels

lymph nodes

The lymphatic system is part of the circulatory system. Besides lymphatic vessels, it consists of small, bean-shaped organs called lymph nodes that are found in groups throughout the body.

The circulatory system includes the cardiovascular system and lymphatic system. The lymphatic system, a key part of the immune system, helps the body fight diseases.

wind through the body like rivers and streams. These vessels constantly move blood in the body.

The cardiovascular system is also part of the circulatory system. The other part of the circulatory system is called the lymphatic system. The lymphatic system carries a fluid called lymph around the body. Lymph helps fight infections and is carried by lymphatic vessels. Small organs called lymph nodes are grouped in certain points along the lymphatic vessels.

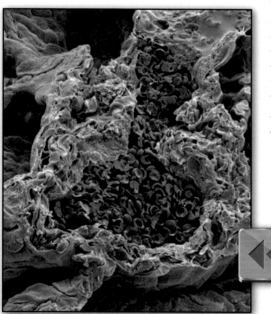

◀◀ A very powerful microscope captured this image of small blood vessels moving blood in a lung.

ARTERIES, CAPILLARIES, AND VEINS

The main vessels are arteries, veins, and capillaries. Arteries carry blood out from the heart. Veins return blood to the heart. Arteries are the thickest of all blood vessels. They expand and contract to keep blood moving away from the heart. Veins contain valves that prevent blood from

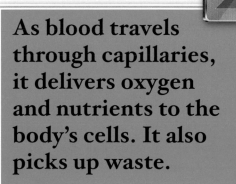

red blood cell carrying oxygen

capillary

red blood cell with no oxygen

to vein

from artery

oxygen

to body's cells

from body's cells

As blood travels through capillaries, it delivers oxygen and nutrients to the body's cells. It also picks up waste.

flowing backward. Capillaries are tiny passages that connect the arteries and the veins to the body's tissues.

In the capillaries, the blood from the arteries transfers oxygen and nutrients to cells in the tissues. The blood in other capillaries collects waste products from the cells. That blood flows into veins and back to the heart.

Veins have valves, which are flaps that can open and shut.

BLOOD WORK

Blood makes up about 8 percent of a human's total body weight. It has many elements in it that help the body perform basic functions.

Blood carries nutrients to cells throughout the body. These nutrients come from food the person eats. The nutrients are fuel for cells to do work. Cells make waste products and blood carries them away. Waste is taken to the kidneys. The kidneys are organs that filter the blood and help remove waste from the body. Cells also produce

◀◀ Blood also carries heat created by muscles and other layers of cells in the circulatory system.

THINK ABOUT IT

Which foods do you think provide your body with the best nutrients: cookies and soda or an apple and milk?

carbon dioxide. Blood carries the carbon dioxide to the lungs, which send it out of the body through breathing.

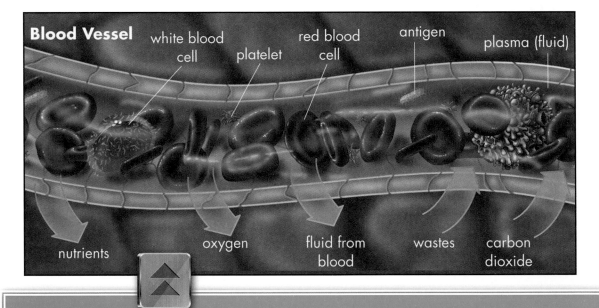

Blood Vessel — white blood cell — platelet — red blood cell — antigen — plasma (fluid)

nutrients | oxygen | fluid from blood | wastes | carbon dioxide

The walls of blood vessels are made up of living cells through which oxygen, nutrients, and waste products can pass into and out of the blood.

Blood Cells

Blood cells make up about 45 percent of the total volume of blood. Most blood cells are made inside bones in a soft, spongy tissue called bone marrow. There are three main kinds of blood cells: red blood cells, white blood cells, and platelets. Red blood cells are the most common. They are round discs with flat centers that look like shallow bowls. One drop of blood contains millions of red blood cells.

Red blood cells move oxygen through the body. In each cell,

A material called bone marrow fills the central part of certain bones. The dark red marrow is where some blood cells are made.

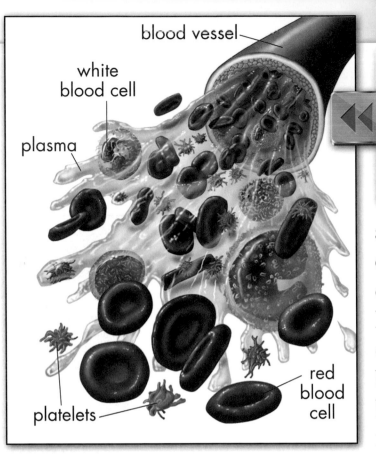

blood vessel

white blood cell

plasma

platelets

red blood cell

Blood is red because there are more red blood cells than white blood cells or platelets.

an iron-rich substance called hemoglobin carries the oxygen. Hemoglobin and oxygen together give blood its red color. Red blood cells last about 120 days before wearing out and dying. Old cells are broken down in the spleen and liver.

THINK ABOUT IT

Oxygen and hemoglobin combine to give blood its red color. Why is the element iron so important to a person's blood?

Blood has far fewer white blood cells than it does red blood cells. Healthy people have about 1 white blood cell for every 700 red blood cells. White blood cells help the body stay healthy. They are part of the immune system, which protects the body from foreign substances called antigens. Antigens can be any foreign material, including harmful germs, certain foods, and bee stings, that cause illness or disease.

When antigens get inside the body, white blood cells fight against them in several ways. Some swallow up the antigens. Others release proteins that attack

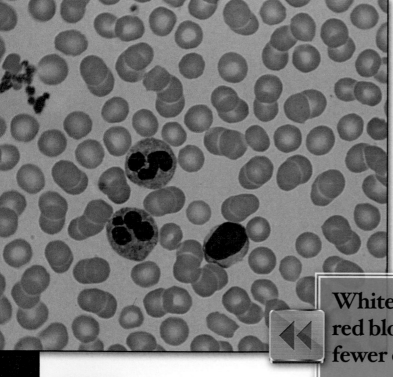

White blood cells are larger than red blood cells, but there are fewer of them in blood.

Some white blood cells attack antigens by swallowing them up.

the antigens. Some white blood cells give off substances that help the immune system attack the antigens.

Other white blood cells help break down and remove dead cells. White blood cells live for less than twenty-four hours in the bloodstream.

COMPARE AND CONTRAST
Red and white blood cells do different tasks. Other than color, how are white blood cells unlike red blood cells?

PLATELETS

Platelets are the smallest type of blood cell. Platelets are more common in blood than white blood cells are, but they are much smaller. Platelets stick to one another and help form blood clots. Clots plug holes in the walls of blood vessels. This clotting helps stop bleeding. Platelets try to keep blood from leaving the vessels. When injured tissue triggers the clotting process,

Platelets, the small pink cells, bind together and help plug wounds in the walls of blood vessels.

THINK ABOUT IT

A bruise happens when blood vessels break and leak blood out under the skin. Why do bruises change color?

the tissue is repaired and the clot fades away. Small holes can clot naturally, but large wounds need more than just platelets to stop bleeding.

The body can make more or fewer platelets when needed.

A purple bruise slowly fades to yellow and other colors as blood breaks down and the injury heals.

21

Plasma

Plasma is the liquid part of blood. It carries the blood cells that move around in the blood. About 92 percent of plasma is water.

Plasma also has other material that help keep the body healthy and fuel cells. Plasma contains many different proteins. It also has nutrients such as fats,

Healthy people can donate plasma. These donations help sick people.

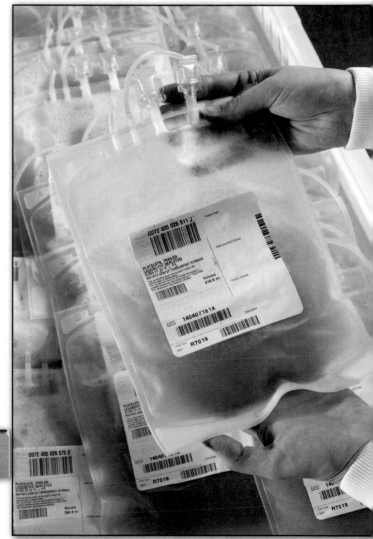

sugars, salts, vitamins, and minerals. Plasma also helps move heat throughout the body. It plays an important role in maintaining normal blood pressure. It also aids in keeping the body's systems working in balance.

THINK ABOUT IT

Plasma helps move heat throughout the body. Why do you think this task is easy for plasma to do?

Another important job plasma has is to move wastes to the kidneys, liver, and lungs, where the body can get rid of them.

Blood Pressure

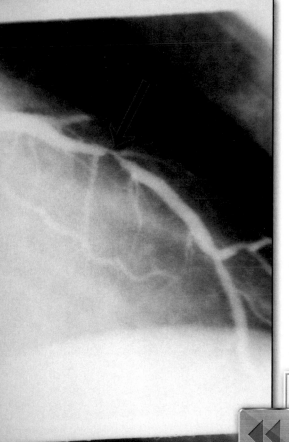

Plasma affects the body's blood pressure, which is measured by listening to thc flow of blood through an artery. The body controls blood pressure through changes in heartbeat and flow of blood through thc heart. When these factors change, blood pressure can be too high or too low.

High blood pressure, or hypertension, can be caused by problems with the flow of blood

A buildup of cholesterol and fats in the arteries can cause them to become narrower, which can result in high blood pressure.

Doctors fix blockages in blood vessels by transplanting, or moving, veins to make new pathways for the blood to flow through. This operation is called **bypass** surgery.

through vessels. When the force of the blood against the walls of the blood vessels is too high, a person has high blood pressure. Cholesterol, a waxy substance in blood plasma, can collect on the inner walls of arteries. Fats and other substances can collect there as well. The deposits can limit blood flow. In severe cases, this can lead to a heart attack because blood cannot flow to the heart.

A **bypass** operation may be used to help prevent heart attacks in people who have large deposits of cholesterol or fat.

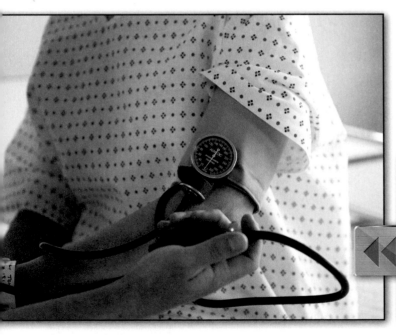

Doctors measure blood pressure using a special instrument that allows them to listen to the rushing sounds of blood.

BLOOD TYPES AND DONORS

The body is always making blood. As a result, some blood can be removed from the body and the body will remain healthy. People can donate blood to help others who are sick or injured. Getting someone else's blood is called a transfusion. People can also donate blood platelets and plasma.

There are four common blood groups, or types: O, A, B, and AB. Each group also has a factor that makes it positive or negative.

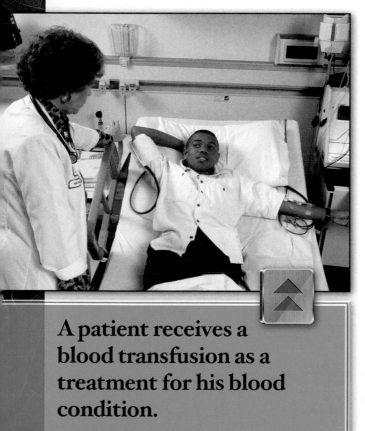

A patient receives a blood transfusion as a treatment for his blood condition.

A person with one blood type usually cannot receive blood from someone with a different blood type. This is because substances called antibodies will attack any cell in the blood that is not usually found in the body. So, a person with type B blood will have anti-A antibodies. That person cannot receive blood from a type A donor. The blood type O can be donated to people with any blood type.

THINK ABOUT IT
Type O blood can be given to people with any blood type. What type of blood can a type O person receive from a blood donor?

People with type AB blood can receive types AB, A, B, or O blood.

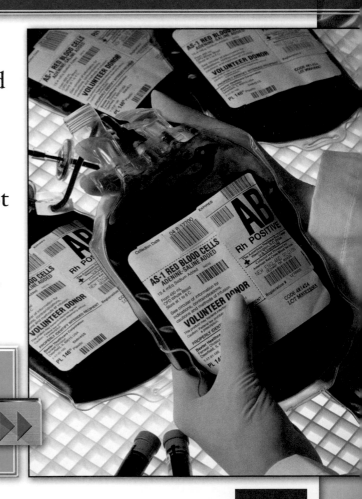

WORKING TOGETHER

The heart, blood vessels, and blood make up the cardiovascular system, which aids many other systems. Blood, the main fluid in humans, helps the lungs in

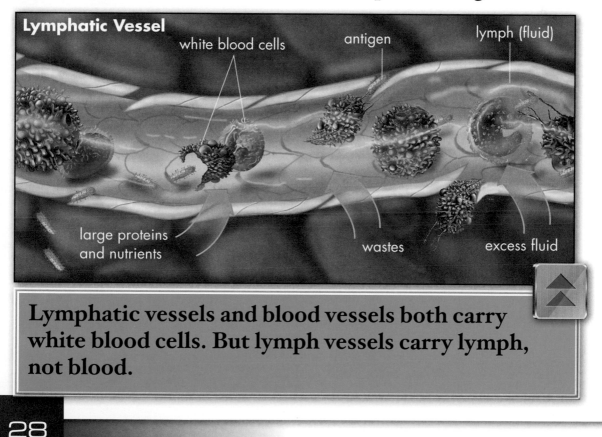

Lymphatic Vessel

white blood cells

antigen

lymph (fluid)

large proteins and nutrients

wastes

excess fluid

Lymphatic vessels and blood vessels both carry white blood cells. But lymph vessels carry lymph, not blood.

COMPARE AND CONTRAST

The cardiovascular and lymphatic systems both circulate fluids throughout the body. What is the chief difference between the two systems?

breathing and the body in removing wastes through the kidneys, spleen, and liver.

The lymphatic system is the other system that makes up the circulatory system. That system carries lymph, a pale fluid that bathes tissues. Lymph is made of white blood cells and a liquid that is like plasma. The lymphatic system helps fight infections in the body. Each system works together to keep the body alive and in balance.

Humans could not live without a healthy heart. Taking care of it and keeping the blood healthy is important to staying in shape and living a long life.

Glossary

antibodies Substances made by special cells of the body that combine with an antigen and fight its effects.

aorta The main artery that carries blood away from the heart to the rest of the body.

arteries Blood vessels that move blood away from the heart.

blood vessels Small tubes that carry blood around the body.

bone marrow Soft matter inside bones where blood cells are made.

capillaries Tiny blood vessels that connect the small arteries and veins to the body's tissues.

chambers Enclosed spaces inside the heart.

diseases Illnesses that stop the body or mind from working correctly.

donate To make a gift of or to contribute.

muscle A body tissue that produces movement.

nutrients Substances that provide the body with what it needs to live and grow.

oxygen An element that is found on Earth and is necessary for life.

proteins Nutrients that the body needs to grow, repair tissues, and stay healthy.

pumps Draws, forces, or drives something onward, such as the heart pumping blood throughout the body.

relaxing Making something less tense, tight, or stiff.

rhythm A regular pattern of movement.

spleen An organ that filters the blood. It destroys worn-out red blood cells and produces some white blood cells.

squeezing Pressing something tightly.

tissues Layers of cells, usually of one kind, that form the basic structural materials of a plant or an animal.

FOR MORE INFORMATION

Books

Ballard, Carol. *What Is My Pulse?* Chicago, IL: Raintree, 2011.

Caster, Shannon. *Heart* (Body Works). New York, NY: Rosen Publishing, 2010.

Jordan, Apple. *My Heart and Blood*. New York, NY: Marshall Cavendish Benchmark, 2012.

Ollhoff, Jim. *The Heart*. Edina, MN: ABDO Publishing, 2012.

Oxlade, Chris. *The Circulatory System: Where Do I Get My Energy?* Chicago, IL: Capstone Raintree, 2014.

Slike, Janet. *Take a Closer Look at Your Heart*. Mankato, MN: The Child's World, 2014.

Storad, Conrad J. *Your Circulatory System*. Minneapolis, MN: Lerner Publications, 2013.

Websites

Because of the changing nature of Internet links, Rosen Publishing has developed an online list of websites related to the subject of this book. This site is updated regularly. Please use this link to access the list:

http://www.rosenlinks.com/LFO/Heart

INDEX